This is a gift from the:

Danville Library Foundation

COOL
Costumes

How to Stage
Your Very Own Show

Karen Latchana Kenney

Consulting Editor, Diane Craig, M.A./Reading Specialist

ABDO
Publishing Company

WITHDRAWN

Note to Adult Helpers

When it comes to putting on a show, costumes are important! To complete the activities in this book, kids will need some supervision, especially when they are using hot glue guns. Show each child how to use a hot glue gun and stick around to help them.

Before beginning, find a good place for kids to make their costumes. Make sure there is a specific cutting area with a cutting mat and scissors. Protect surfaces with newspaper or an old sheet. If kids are scrounging around for materials, remind them to get permission from an adult before they alter the fabric or clothing they are using for their costumes.

If kids want to purchase materials, help them set a budget. Remind them that they also need to clean up after making their projects. And, finally, don't forget to encourage kids as they create their cool costumes!

Visit us at www.abdopublishing.com

Published by ABDO Publishing Company, 8000 West 78th Street, Edina, Minnesota 55439. Copyright © 2010 by Abdo Consulting Group, Inc. International copyrights reserved in all countries. No part of this book may be reproduced in any form without written permission from the publisher. The Checkerboard Library™ is a trademark and logo of ABDO Publishing Company.

Printed in the United States.
Design and Production: Colleen Dolphin, Mighty Media, Inc.
Photo Credits: Colleen Dolphin, Shutterstock, iStockphoto (Zsolt Biczó, Ronald Bloom, Michal Koziarski)
Series Editor: Katherine Hengel, Pam Price
Activity Production: Britney Haeg

The following manufactures/names appearing in this book are trademarks: Crayola® Washable Glitter Glue, Elmer's® Glue-All™, Office Depot® Posterboard, Scribbles® Dimensional Fabric Paint, Target® Aluminum Foil and Tulip® Soft Fabric Paint™

Library of Congress Cataloging-in-Publication Data

Kenney, Karen Latchana.
  Cool costumes : how to stage your very own show / Karen Latchana Kenney.
    p. cm. -- (Cool performances)
  Includes webliography and index.
  ISBN 978-1-60453-714-7
  1. Costume--Juvenile literature. 2. Theater--Juvenile literature. I. Title.

PN2067.K46 2010
792.02'6--dc22
                                      2009001751

Get the Picture!

There are many activities and how-to photos in this title. Each how-to photo has a color border around it, so match the border color to the appropriate activity step!

 activity step →

Contents

CREATING COOL PERFORMANCES

What's it all about?

Imagine putting on your very own show! Performing in front of an **audience** sounds fun, right? It is! You can pretend to be anything you want to be. Create an **illusion** through your costume, makeup, and stage. Tell a story by acting out a script. Put everything together, and you have a cool show!

You can create many kinds of shows. You can tell a funny story or a serious story. Put on a musical or a fairy tale. Creep out your audience with a monster or a ghost story. You can even be an alien on a strange planet!

Cool Performances Series

Cool Costumes	Cool Scripts & Acting
Cool Makeup	Cool Sets & Props
Cool Productions	Cool Special Effects

Permission

Be sure you have permission from an adult to put on a show. Ask for permission before you paint or cut materials. It is important to know that the sheets or clothes you are using are old and unwanted! Make sure you also have permission to use a hot glue gun.

Safety

To make your costumes, you will need a large, flat surface like a floor or a table. Protect this surface by laying down some newspaper or an old sheet. Always use a cutting board underneath whatever you are cutting. Be careful with those sharp scissors and hot glue guns!

Clean Up

Remember to clean up when you are done! Use a vacuum to get the bits of fabric that may have fallen on the floor. Wipe down the surface you worked on. Also, take care of the great costumes you just made! Make sure they are clean. Then fold and store them in a plastic tub or bin.

Show Styles

There are many show styles. Shows can be one style or a combination of styles. Here are just a few.

Drama

Emotions are important in a drama. A dramatic show might be sad or it could make audiences laugh!

Fairy Tale

Fairy tales teach lessons. They have make-believe characters such as fairies, unicorns, and goblins.

Fantasy

Imaginary creatures make this kind of show fantastic! Mad scientists create monsters in laboratories, and aliens fly through space!

Musical

Singing is just as important as acting in a musical. Songs tell parts of the story.

GETTING DRESSED

Part of getting into character involves looking like your character! Combined with acting skills and makeup, a costume makes your character more believable to an **audience**. Costumes can make you look like you are from another time. Or they can turn you into some kind of creature. However costumes are used, they are fun to make and wear in a show!

Making sure your costume suits your part is important. Look at the **setting** of the script. Is it in **medieval** or modern times? Read the description of your character. Is your character poor or rich? Young or old? Put these pieces together to create a costume that fits your character.

6

Costumes have always played an important part in theater. Masks can show age or emotion. In ancient Greece, male actors often wore masks that made them look like female characters. They did this because women were not allowed to act on stage.

Today, costume designers study scripts to create costumes for professional shows. Then they research the clothing worn during the play's time frame to create **period** costumes. They might make unique costumes for fantasy characters. Costume designers work with directors to make sure the costumes fit the show.

Designing costumes for your show is a lot of fun! You can make a simple costume with just a mask. Or you can go all out! Just have fun and make your costume as cool as it can be!

A PATTERN TO FOLLOW

Things to know before you begin

When it comes to making costumes, the possibilities are endless! Look for old items at home or in a thrift store. Use hats, jewelry, and old clothes to become any kind of character you want. You just need a little imagination and creativity!

You can also make costumes using some basic tools and materials. A hot glue gun and an old sheet may be all that you need to put together your costume. The activities in this book will show you how.

Look for costume materials at craft and fabric stores. These stores will have big selections of fabric, ribbon, and crafting supplies. Many fabric stores have bins of fabric **remnants**. These are small pieces of fabric sold at a discount. Check out garage sales and thrift stores for old sheets, tablecloths, and curtains. You can use the material from them to make some cool costumes!

STAGE KIT

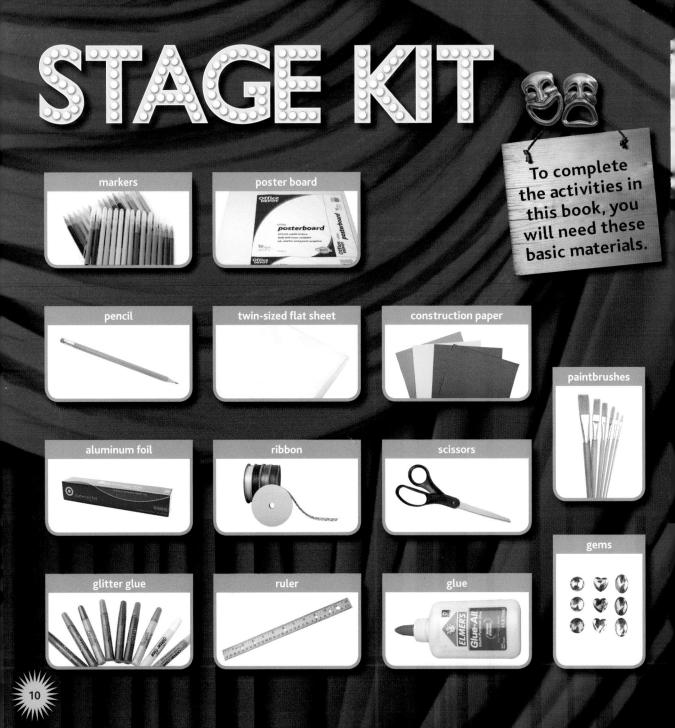

To complete the activities in this book, you will need these basic materials.

markers

poster board

pencil

twin-sized flat sheet

construction paper

paintbrushes

aluminum foil

ribbon

scissors

gems

glitter glue

ruler

glue

10

cardboard

white T-shirt

measuring tape

glow-in-the-dark 3D paint

paper towel tube

black T-shirt

sequins

headband

stapler

black elastic

fabric paints

white elastic

yarn

tulle

fabric remnants

felt

hot glue gun

fake fur

paper plate

hole punch

Regal Robe

Turn an old sheet into a **majestic** robe! Real kings and queens wear robes made from fancy materials such as fur, soft velvet, and silk. See how fancy you can make your robe look!

STAGE KIT

- twin-sized flat sheet
- scissors
- measuring tape
- yarn
- fabric paints
- fabric remnants
- hot glue gun

1 Fold the sheet in half so that the top end touches the bottom end. Cut the sheet in half as shown. Do not cut along the fold!

2 Measure how big around your neck is. Double the measurement and cut a piece of yarn to that length. Run the yarn underneath the fold. This is your robe!

3 Decorate one side of your robe with fabric paints and fabric **remnants**. Try squares or stars! Attach the fabric shapes with a hot glue gun.

4 Tie the yarn around your neck and check out your new robe!

Show Stoppers

You can use this robe for other characters too!
- add a cone-shaped hat and a wand to be a magician
- wear a **leotard** under it to be a superhero

13

Swirly Skirt

Float on air in this fun skirt! Make it from tulle, a type of netting named for a city in France. Your skirt will be extra fluffy with this cool material!

STAGE KIT

- 2 yards (2 m) of tulle
- scissors
- measuring tape
- 2 feet (0.6 m) of white elastic
- ribbons (optional)

1. Decide what color tulle you would like to use. If you want two colors, use 1 yard (1 m) of each color.

2. Lay the tulle out and cut it into strips. The strips should be about 4 inches (10 cm) wide and 1 yard (1 m) long.

3. Cut a piece of elastic that you can tie comfortably around your waist.

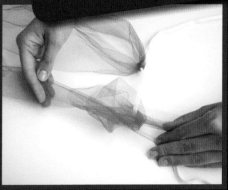

4. Tie the strips of tulle around the elastic. You can use single knots. Don't put strips too close to the ends of the elastic. You will need to be able to tie the ends together.

5. Fluff out the tulle to make your skirt full. If you want, add some ribbon. Tie your skirt around your waist. You look stunning!

T-Shirt Transformers

Turn plain T-shirts into great costumes! A T-shirt can become a sports uniform, a **tuxedo** shirt, or even a skeleton!

STAGE KIT
- white T-shirt
- cardboard
- fabric paint
- paintbrush

1 Put a piece of cardboard inside a white T-shirt. The cardboard stops the paint from bleeding through to the other side of the shirt.

2 Paint your team name and number on the front of the shirt. Then paint vertical stripes down the front of the T-shirt.

3 On the back, write your number in large numerals in the middle. Write your character's last name in capital letters above the number. Add vertical stripes if you like.

Show Stoppers

Try making a football uniform! Paint your number on the front of the shirt in the middle. Use large numerals. Write your team name above the number. On the back, paint your number again. Write your character's last name above the number.

STAGE KIT

- white T-shirt
- cardboard
- fabric paint
- paintbrush

 1 Put a piece of cardboard inside a white T-shirt.

2 On the front, paint a bow tie just under the collar.

3 Paint six squiggly lines down the front of the shirt.

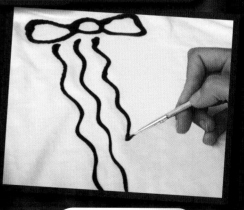

TUXEDO SHIRT

4 Add an old suit jacket and you have a **tuxedo**!

SKELETON

1 Put a piece of cardboard inside a black T-shirt.

2 Use glow-in-the-dark 3D paint to draw the bones. First paint two lines down the front of the shirt. They should go from the collar to the bottom. Make them 2 inches (5 cm) apart. This is the skeleton's spine!

3 Now it's time to make the ribs. Use the 3D paint to make ten ribs. The ends should curve slightly upward. Try to space the ribs evenly along the spine. Wear some black pants to finish the look. Spooky!

19

Pirate Patch

Felt makes a good eye patch because it is stiff. To make felt, **fibers** are pressed together into a thick mat.

1 Cut a triangle out of black felt. Use the scissors to round each point. This is your eye patch.

2 Use a pencil to poke holes in two of the corners of the patch. Cut a piece of elastic. It should be long enough to fit around your head.

3 Tie one end of the elastic to each hole. Put on your patch. Arrr!

Slimy Scales

STAGE KIT

- 9 x 12 inch (23 x 30 cm) pieces of craft felt in different colors
- scissors
- T-shirt
- hot glue gun

1 Cut out small circles from the felt. Make them between 1 to 2 inches (3 to 5 cm) in diameter.

2 Attach the circles to the T-shirt with the glue gun. Start with a row of circles along the bottom. The circles should overlap slightly. Try alternating colors.

3 Attach another row of circles right above the first row. The circles should slightly overlap the first row. Stagger the circles so they don't line up exactly.

Mighty Medallion

STAGE KIT

- pencil
- posterboard
- scissors
- aluminum foil
- tape
- hole punch
- ribbon
- gems
- sequins
- glue

1 Draw a circle on a piece of poster board. Cut out the circle. This is your **medallion**!

2 Cover the medallion with aluminum foil. Tape the ends of the aluminum foil to the back. Punch a hole at the top and thread some ribbon through the hole. Tie the ends together. Glue some gems and sequins on the front!

Glitzy Bracelets

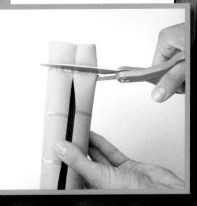

1 Cut the paper towel tube lengthwise with a scissors. Next, cut the tube crosswise as shown. These are your bracelets!

2 Decorate the bracelets. Use paint, glitter glue, and markers. Use a hot glue gun to attach ribbon, sequins, and gems.

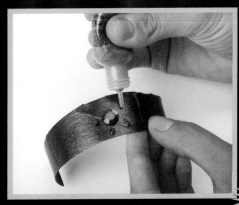

23

Royal Heads

Kings and queens often wear crowns. But a princess usually wears a hennin, which is a cone-shaped hat with strips of ribbon or fabric flowing from the top.

PRINCESS HENNIN

1 Roll a piece of construction paper into a cone. Make sure the bottom is large enough to fit around your head. Staple the paper in the cone shape.

2 Decorate the outside with markers and glitter glue. Try gluing on sequins or gems. Tuck some ribbon through the top of the hat and tape it to the inside.

24

CLASSY CROWN

1 Cut a strip of poster board that is 2 inches (5 cm) wide. It should be long enough to fit around your head. Make sure the ends overlap so you can staple them together later.

2 Cut a piece of construction paper that is 4 inches (10 cm) wide. It should be as long as the poster board piece. Glue it to the poster board.

3 Cut a zigzag edge along the top of the construction paper. Gently bend the poster board into a ring that fits on your head. Staple the ends.

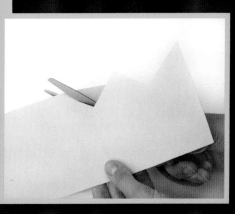

4 Decorate the crown with markers and glitter glue. Glue on aluminum foil stars, gems, or sequins. Make it sparkle!

Funky Glasses

Cool glasses add a lot of character! Depending on the style, glasses can make a character seem smart, old, glamorous, or nerdy.

1 Lay the ruler across the poster board. Make a mark at 4 inches (10 cm). Make a second mark at 6 inches (15 cm). Make a third mark at 8 inches (20 cm). Make a fourth mark at 12 inches (30 cm).

top

left

4 in   6 in   8 in   12 in

2 Draw faint vertical lines over each of your marks.

3 Draw your glasses as shown. Color them with a marker and cut them out. Fold back the earpieces and put on your glasses!

Mask Mania

Use paper plates to make a variety of masks. Don't forget to make holes for your eyes!

1 Draw a face on a paper plate. Make sure you will be able to see out of the eyes!

2 Cut out the eye holes and decorate your mask however you like! Try markers and paints. If you want to add animal ears, cut them out of poster board and staple them to the top of the plate.

3 Punch a hole on each side of your mask. Tie one end of the elastic to each hole. Now put on your mask!

Animal Ears

What creature will you become? An animal, a monster, or maybe an alien? Make the ears as wild as you want!

STAGE KIT

- scissors
- poster board
- ruler
- fake fur
- hot glue gun
- fabric paint
- paintbrush
- headband

1

To make pointy ears, cut two triangles out of poster board. Fold the bottoms of the triangles as shown. The fold should be as wide as the headband. There should be about 1 inch (3 cm) below the fold.

2

Now decorate your ears with fake fur. Do not decorate below the fold! Use a hot glue gun to attach the fake fur to the triangles. You can use fabric paint to add the inner ear.

3

Put glue on the backs of the folds. Press the fold of each ear under the headband. You're an instant animal!

Show Stoppers

Become a wacky monster or an alien by attaching strange shapes to the headband. Try lightning bolts, giant screws, or stars!

29

CONCLUSION

How did your costumes turn out? Costumes can be a big part of a show. Use what you have learned from these activities to design your own unique costumes. Let your creativity flow and see what kind of look you can create! Your creations can really make your show sparkle.

But you need more than costumes to put on a great show. Check out the other books in the Cool Performances series to learn more about putting on a show. Try some fun makeup to complete your look. Practice your acting skills and try writing a script. Create a super set and add special effects. Take it all on stage and put on a cool show!

GLOSSARY

audience – a group of people watching a performance.

fiber – a thread-like part.

illusion – something that looks real but is not.

leotard – a tight one-piece outfit.

majestic – royal, or showing power and beauty.

medallion – a piece of jewelry that is shaped like a medal.

medieval – of or belonging to the Middle Ages, which was the period from AD 500 to 1500.

period – relating to a particular time in history.

remnant – a small bit that remains after the rest is gone.

setting – the place where a story happens.

tuxedo – a man's dressy jacket, usually black, worn with a white shirt and bow tie.

INDEX